My Life In Poem

WILLA D. JONES

ISBN-13: 978-1479263059

Contents

Believe It

Believe it when you see someone bundled up sleeping in the street

Believe it when you see someone looking in the garbage for food to eat

Believe it 'cause all of these things are real and none are made up

Believe that there are many men, women and children who are down on their luck

Believe that with the economy all twisted and headed straight to hell

Believe that there are many who just give up, commit suicide or take leave for a jail cell

Believe that to the homeless, jail with three hot meals, cell buddies for friends and a cot

Believe to some may mean nothing but to the homeless means one hell of a lot

Believe with faith all things are possible for all including you and me

Believe in God, have faith, and pray, then change will come all you have to do is believe

Off the Street – Anna Louise Inn

Halt! Freeze! Stop! Off the street I heard a voice say

The voice within me was loud and clear, I obeyed and I'm off the street today

Being homeless for five years I grew to know the street therefore I became bored

I longed for a change in the ways of my life so my determination began to soar

After Pathways, Talbert House, Bethany House, The Drop Inn Center and finally to jail

The change in my life became mandatory and I realized that only I could pay in order to bail

I remembered while on the street I heard about this place called The Anna Louise Inn

I remembered I heard I'd have to have a job and pay the first month's rent with deposit right then

Somebody said that if you're looking to get some real help go to the Off The Street Program

They told me that the program was in the Anna Louise Inn on Lytle and I said, "Well I just be damned!!"

I decided to call this Off The Street Program located inside the Anna Louise Inn

I found out how to get there which was the best of my life to rid myself of anger, hatred and sin

I found the stability I forgot I had, they gave me my own room but I had to earn my key

I had my first sense of obtaining a goal in over five years, please believe me!!

I earned my room key and opened my ears, I heard scholars who had beat their addictions

Their stories were my own so I knew to listen to them I'd find a cure for my affliction

I finally got a job and started to save my money, I looked forward to move into the Inn

I was glad when the facilitators of O.T.S. told me I was graduating I thanked God for my life again

So I say to all women, teenagers whether blind, crippled or crazy, that the Anna Louise Inn is the best

They were always there to help women in their transition, always welcoming all their guests

Their hands of love and understanding went out further when The Off The Street Program came

So to ridicule these people for helping and saving so many from the street I honestly feel it's a shame

So I pray for the place that means so much to me as it does to countless others too

I pray that God will intervene in this senseless fight as I pray to God that they never have to move!!

The Graduate

Today is a very important day for you

Today is the beginning of a new life, so to yourself be true

Today is the day that you leave your past behind

Today is the day that you can finally see your future begin to shine

Today only you can open the doors to the rest of your life

Today forget, but always remember your past never forgetting the toils and the strife

Today you graduate into a world that is old to some but for you it will be all brand new

Today thank God and keep his word in your heart no matter what you do

So say good-bye to the past and to the devil with his wicked ways

Say hello to a new beginning and never forget to pray

A Gift of Sorrow

There was love, peace and happiness on my side

One man with me for twenty years, just my kind

He had asked me to marry him three times, each time I said
no

Not knowing that time was running out for us as we go

He became ill with high blood pressure and then had a
stroke

I had everything I needed but when he died he left me broke

I went from the house, to the car and even the pool in the
back

To being homeless, eating trash and even smoking crack

I tried living with people I knew back when times were good

It would never last being an outcast and so misunderstood

I tried homeless shelters with beds and eating solid food

But shelters have curfews and I wasn't for following the
rules

I found myself all alone hungry and sleeping in the street

I lost everything, only the clothes on my back could I keep

My grief for the loss of my man had turned to sorrow for
myself

I knew there was a lesson in this hand I had been dealt

I started to pray and read the Bible all of the time

Asking God to help me to soothe my aching mind

I began to find strength with new feelings and new ideas

I stopped smoking crack, drinking and got my head clear

I went to a shelter for the homeless, addicts and prostitutes

I found strength to bite my tongue and do what I had to do

I went to A.A. and N.A. meetings and talked out loud

To hear my story let me know that a change was in my cloud

I finally graduated and was able to rent my own room

Got a job, got healthy and my spirit went up to the moon

I started talking to the Lord in song and in prayer everyday

And he turned my sorrow into a gift of life I'm proud to say

So to have sorrow or to feel pity on oneself all of the time

Will take you nowhere but down that wrong and narrow
line

You must look up and recognize where you need to be going

And ask God to help you understand what it is your heart is
sowing

Just remember a gift of sorrow can be a very powerful lesson

And as long as you have faith and believe in God, you will receive his blessings!!

My Father's House

In my Father's house there are many mansions

Many mansions, with many rooms to rest and pray in

In good times, in bad times, day, night, sleep or wake times

All the time I spend in my Father's house 'cause his house is mines

When I was homeless, a drunkard, a drug addict and all alone

I found much comfort and peace just praising in song

When I was hungry, hair nappy, dirty and smelling really bad

I held onto my sanity, when my belief in prayer was all I had

As in any house with rules, my Father has commandments of ten

Even though I would make mistakes, I'd always repent of my sins

And ask for forgiveness with the understanding to make a change

A change for the best so there would be no more fear or pain

Taking what each day brings in prayer and always believe

Having faith to know that my Father's will is best for me

While searching for God's love, wisdom and understanding

I come into the realization of just what my heart was demanding

I began to go to church to learn more about my Father's house

I found peace and my soul was saved I could finally announce

I learned that there is a place in my Father's house for everyone

The young, the old, the lost and the sick at heart and mind

I learned the mistakes I'd made were all of one kind

I understand today that we must learn from the mistakes we've made

And know only by the grace of God can our souls be saved

So won't you come visit in the house of my Father?

Learn the Bible and know that with my Father there is no other

Take your time and search your soul to truly find yourself

And understand that in our Father's house is where we'll be forever safe with plenty of help

Spring

Spring has always been my favorite out all four seasons

Spring has no snow and not too much heat, may that be the reason

Spring with its so many misinterpretations and misunderstandings

Spring to the light so we can see just what mankind is demanding

Spring to the facts: Unemployment and homelessness on the rise, can these things be an illusion

Spring into the reality: We as a people trying to control each other, now this is the confusion

Spring into new horizons, now living with new politicians, new fights and new killings

Spring into arrest which means nothing today for the facts state the state is doing the stealing

Spring to the wake up call so I sprung up one morning and realized my season had come

Spring into the real understanding that the battles only God has won

Spring is the understanding that like all things that come and go, spring is here

Spring back to know that all men are created equal is that not what should be made so clear

Spring to the knowledge that we as people have choices and can make positive decisions

Spring into the word of God and believe with faith, with trust only then can we stop these collisions!

Remembering

Do you ever think of the days of the past?

Do you ever think those being the good days, why they couldn't last?

Remembering when we were children doing everything our elders said

Remembering eating breakfast, lunch, dinner and even what time it was for bed

As time passed some of us traded going to church for drinking beer and wine

Some of us grew up and changed so fast that we just simply ignored the signs

As time passed everything changed all the rules even people, places and things

But time goes on carrying us with it, and we know it can't end until the fat lady sings!

So we keep going on trying to keep up with time and losing our sense of being free

Today we never forget to lock our door, windows and try never to go out alone, you see!

So much robbing, back stabbing, short changing and all of the senseless killings

I love to let my mind drift to the past because the present is so hard dealing!

So for me taking my memory back as far as I can

Keeps me in tune and my eyes open to the future as I pray for people all over God's land!

Ode to the Security of the Fifth Floor

I think back when I first saw my apartment on the fifth floor

I recall feeling relieved, good and happy finally moving in.
Then I heard the opening of the door.

Right then I figured I had moved into a good, quiet and safe
place

Or else I had moved on the wrong side where nothing
would be sacred not even in my space

But as the years passed and we grew into neighbors learning
to respect one another

I learned that we on the fifth floor had the only real security
who was my neighbor, a black brother

As long as my neighbor was here I never had to worry about
strangers hanging around on my floor

As long as my neighbor was here I never worried about
unwanted guests knocking on my door

Since I've learned that all good things often come to an
abrupt end

I realize now that I will forever remember and I will miss my
Neighbor, my Security and my Friend

So may God bless you and keep you always and forever
more

And may he bless you with the job you do so well being security for heaven's front door…

REST IN PEACE MICHAEL TOMBS

Love One Gone

There is time for everything including a time to say hello
and a time for saying goodbye

There is a place for everything including a place to laugh, to
cry and ask for reasons why

To live each day surrounded by the people we love, never
forgetting God is a blessing

Is to know that having a mind to remember precious
moments will always be a lesson

We as people tend to hurt when things don't go our way or
grieve for things that are lost

We as people must keep in mind there is never nothing lost
as long as God is the boss

We must teach our children that as long as we remember
nothing ever really goes away

Teach them the truth about life and death and remember our
experiences everyday

Just remember that the good times always out weight the
bad times

And remember even though people aren't with us they're in
God's House and that's fine!

Lifted

The year being almost gone, I find myself remembering yesterday and looking way back

Thinking of my accomplishments, my failures, not to mention what I need to keep my life on track

Days, months, years go by so fast especially when I believed that I was too busy

Being older today trying to remember where I was, now that memory can make anybody dizzy

The Good, the Bad, don't forget the UGLY, come to life and they are no longer movies on a T.V.

The Good, the Bad and the Ugly becomes a DEATH, DEFYING ACT! Please Believe Me!!

To have shot dope, to have snorted dope and just today understand what it is to be homeless

To have sold dope, drank with the best, went to jail for dope. Looking back, I was so boneless!!!

Today I am looking back, trying to remember what happened and why. Who was in Control?

Again, today looking back, remembering I couldn't but today I don't have parole

Right now, today I praise God for so many blessing. Those I see and those I don't!

 I PRAY GOD LIFTS ME AND SAVES MY SOUL!

Intoxication

Intoxication is being drunk if only for a little while

Intoxication can become a bad habit with a crooked smile

Being high and drunk all alone really makes no sense

Being homeless, a panhandler and a drunk can be a bad defense

The fear of not knowing what your next move can possibly be

Can be intoxicating without a drink, please believe me

The fear of failure constantly day in and day out

Can be an eye opener to a drunk to make a change, no doubt

Once you realize that there is another way to live everyday

To work, maintain your money and eventually find a place to stay

Things start to fall in order for you surely but slowly

As you start to make a change in your life ever so boldly

Intoxicating thoughts will no longer be able to hold you back

Understanding that with the help of God you can get your life on track

So don't stay intoxicated by the fears of the world today

Go to church, read the Bible and get on your knees and pray!

Hoolieo

I ain't Hoolieo I heard somebody say

I ain't out here conning and tricking people for a raise in pay

I'm trying to give others respect as I want for myself

I'm trying to keep my livelihood open to the hand I've been dealt

I ain't Hoolieo I heard another person say

I ain't making up fairy tales trying to get sympathy for money today

I'm trying to be honest to people I meet along the street

I'm trying to receive God's blessing with each heart beat

I ain't Hoolieo I finally shouted very clear out loud

I rebuke thee Hoolieo and vanish thee from my mind up to the clouds

So if things are not going your way and you feel a Hoolieo attack coming on

An urge to con, trick or lie to people for pay, just kick Hoolieo to the curb and curse the day he was born!!

Gone

Gone are the days that we once knew

Gone are the days never to return so now what's new?

Gone is like tomorrow that never comes, it's always today

Gone is the employment rate and housing for people like me, for a change I pray!

Gone are the days of Martin Luther King, John F. Kennedy and singer Luther Vandross

Today some people scream Osama bin Laden is dead as the world yells Barack Obama is the boss

Today we as human people should not be worried or confused as to who is ruling

Today we must understand that this is God's world. So why do the people keep fooling?

I say stop killing ourselves when it is without a doubt we live in order to die

So why not take each day as a blessing above ground and just say hello and when we're gone just say goodbye

Can You

Can you shut 'em down? Does the world believe that this is the world's solution?

Can you shut 'em down? Keeping factories open with no work, now that's pollution

Can you shut 'em down? The free clinics, people homeless, no more Drop Inn Center

Can you shut 'em down? Washington Park, the sanitation workers, I can't help but litter

Can you shut 'em down? Over the Rhine was white then it was black, I thought we were all together

Can you shut 'em down? I'm confused so tell Congress I really thought they knew better

Can you believe in your heart that the decisions of our country are either Republican or Democrat?

Can you believe that out of all the people in the world two simple parties be worthy of so much static?

Can you close your eyes to the reality of the fear that has such a tight grip on our nation today?

Can you keep living shut down and shut up? I'm baffled but not lost for words I can honestly say

For me, learning to live without doubt or fear in my life and keeping God so close to my heart

I have no doubt that without God's blessings this world is doomed to fall completely apart

With much faith and without any regards for the Republicans or Democrats controlling my being

Without any doubt whatsoever today I know that almighty God is the only real thing

So can you shut 'em down? Now slow down and take the time to think, what do you really understand?

You need to come back into the days of Adam and Eve and remember when only God ruled the land!

Appreciation

Appreciation is a word that can be reckoned with

Appreciation is something we often times consider a myth

Appreciation is something I give to God each day for my living above ground

And for His blessing of putting people in my life so stable and sound

To understand just what it is that I as a person need to honestly appreciate

And to know that my mission of appreciation will not be a simple piece of cake

Through being jailed and being homeless not to mention in the world all by myself

I've learned to appreciate the hand that God has gracefully dealt

I've learned to never forget the past and look forward to each day even though not promised

I've learned to forgive but not forget and stop being a doubting Thomas

I recognize and therefore appreciate the changes my life have ultimately taken

I've learned to appreciate my faults for without them there would be no lesson

I've learn to recognize my shortcomings and now I
appreciate God's Almighty Blessings

A Theft In The Economy

It takes a thief to steal the people of the country's belief

It takes a thief to have the people have to change their lives, now that's deep

It takes a thief to double the price of football stadiums and fields

It takes a thief to convince the county the police deserve a Las Vegas deal

It takes a thief to steal channels from our children, scanning for the T.V.

Whether it be for the Converter Box, Cable Box or Direct T.V. Do you understand me?

For me to steal anything or to be classified as a political thief

Would for me never to have believed in the Constitution and damn Democracy

So now where do we go as a people in order to regain the stability we so freely lost?

In the future we must read every dotted line, keep the faith and let God alone be the boss!

A Peaceful Place

There's a place I go to on different days of every week

Where I can learn about making things that all kinds of people seek

I learn to make jewelry; I learn how to knit and to even play with clay

I learn all sorts of things and if I want, I can stay and learn all day

This place is open to women from all walks of everyday life

In this place you can find peace of mind from the world's toils and strife

We come together and talk to find solutions for so many different problems

As we knit and make jewelry we pray for God's help with our problems to be able to solve them

This place is called the Sarah Center here in downtown Vine Street

Who would ever believe this place of peace would be located right off the downtown beat

I have been blessed to find the Sarah Center and meet all the Sarah Center Girls

I just wish that there were more places of this stature all over the world

So I hope I can just pass the blessing on to those who may be lonely and bored

And be able to open the door to those lost souls who feel their being ignored

Come into the Sarah Center and meet all the many women of different cultures and pray

That your day may be fulfilled by the grace of God in the Sarah Center each and everyday

A Friend

To be called a friend is sometimes very hard to be

To be a friend is an honor with many responsibilities

To have a friend is someone you can depend on

To have a friend with you when all hope is gone

Being human beings we all fall short of God's grace

Being human plus a friend can be a difficult race

Due to difficult circumstances in every person's life

To put trust and faith in someone can be only strife

So for me I keep the faith and never forget to pray

As I sing that old hymn "What a Friend We Have in Jesus"

Each and every day!!

A Message To My Son

Now that God has laid you down to sleep. No wrong word, he has laid you down to die,

Although God made this day for us he knew that your family and friends would cry

We all live life and life is good. But we also know that death is inevitable and the end must come

We also know how we got here but we don't how we're getting out, whether the battle has been lost or won

 I will rejoice because I know in my heart that you've experienced God's love, now it's time to hear his voice

He said, even though brief, your life here is done and for you to come on home

No longer to walk all over God's heaven but to be in his kingdom and forever let your spirit roam

Even though you're gone and out of my view, we will always be together in my mind, heart and soul

And for as long as I live, seeing you again in eternal peace together will be forever my blessed gold

All praise due to God life will still go on. But to that I was your mother, that's enough to keep me strong

Remembering the love we shared and the understanding of God's love there is no way I could possibly go wrong

You have gone before me and I am left here to live and learn for I know that eventually it will be my turn to go home

But until then I will live life, pray and always remember the love we had all through my journey no matter how long

So may your soul be forever with the Lord for the Bible say he is the only one that will give you rest

Even though our life together was cut short I pray every day that you know I gave you my all, my best

Just rest assured that you will be missed and forever loved, only God knows just how much

So just go with God remembering me and look forward to the day I will see you again as our spirit finally touch...

Love forever,

Your Mother

The Prediction

What would you do if you could predict your every
tomorrow?

Remembering that tomorrow never comes it's always today,
now that can bring some sorrow

Thinking of the changes that the people of the world are
being subjected to

Remembering the days of the past is what I'll always cherish
for thinking today can be oh so cruel

Today there is a complete new set of words we as a people
must learn

Words like: Shut 'em down, unemployment rising, evictions
and homelessness, now I'm concerned

So do you believe that we could make a change in this world
If we could predict our future?

Believe me being either a Democrat, a Republican or a
Socialist we all come up a loser

Believe that this is God's world, somehow the world seems
to have forgotten

Believe if we as mankind don't come back to God we'll all be
lost, burned up and then turn rotten

To be able to predict tomorrow or for me to be a psychic
honestly is not my choice

Now predict the readings of the Bible about God's return, I believe it's time for the politicians to heed to God's voice!!!

The Struggle

What was all of the fighting for human rights really for?

Why struggle for rights when half of the world is wrong? Now that's an eye sore!

What are the marchers saying or what's the boycotts all about?

Why do the people still cry for "Jesus to help"? For in God people know there's no doubt

What does being homeless have to do with all these dilemmas?

Why do the homeless get beat while the wrong go free just to be later called a killer?

Today we as a people still have control of all our choices and decisions

So today let's not forget the past, the marches, the boycotts or we'll be in a collision

Collision course with the good, the bad, the ugly and the black and white syndrome

Collision course of who can do better or why should I help the person who's all alone

We must never forget we all live one day at a time so we must live just for today

We need never forget no matter how we live in this life, we all will die anyway!

So since we all have that same common ground which is six feet deep

Forgive the past and recognize that our future with God's blessing is what we need!!!

The Understanding

Understanding today about life and its meaning have come a very long way with me. I had to come into the understanding that there was nothing outside myself that could make my life better! I had to understand that I have a choice. To know that I was no longer incarcerated by my own being and no longer restricted by my own soul! I could either come into the realization that to live is right now because death is inevitable!!

We as adults can never forget that growing up as children everything was external. As children we were nothing more than human sponges!! Therefore whatever the adults in our childhood fed us, we trustily ate. I believe that what they fed us became our internal instincts.

Through my growing, school, jail, being homeless, I eventually came to the understanding of the meaning of choice. I had to understand that there is none other like me, only I could make the changes necessary to allow my uniqueness to shine. For I am unique! One of a kind! Understanding my uniqueness, understanding I have choices in this world only justified my decision to live and not die!

These realizations seemed to wake up my self esteem and many positive aspects for me. I suddenly remembered that I did go to church, I remembered some of the best teachings of the Bible whether it was about Moses or Mohammad. My understanding of life today is G.O.D. meaning: *Good Orderly Direction!!*

I understand today that to live now is my only necessity, for why kill myself or commit suicide when death for all is a sure thing. It's gonna happen! To live is a job and I take it on with great pride. Keep in mind that you are the most important one and to know your size, your height, your weight, hair color and so forth is what makes you. So my meaning is my understanding that:

I Am Unique

I Am Blessed

I Am Living Until Death Do Me Part

Too Comfortable

Have you ever had days where everything seems to be
alright

Have you ever had days where your last problem seemed
out of sight

Have you ever had days where you thought you were at
your very best

And in that same day you felt a wet mop slap you back into
a mess

Those are the days that I be mindful of everyday and all of
the time

I've learned that with the good days I must not forget the
bad days, they're all mine!

For me I believe that the luxury of living and being able to
make a conscious choice

To know right from wrong, to make decisions and to take
heed to God's voice

Keeps me in tune to the understanding that living life can be
very good

And in past experiences I've been blessed so I try to live life
as I should

I've come into the understanding of what living life should
be all about

I've learned to believe in miracles, believe in blessings and God's love no doubt!

Just take the time to think about these words while you're looking for that lucky day

Consider these words that the good and bad days are what you make them

Just remember that I pray!!!!

What's Going On

What's going on asked singer Marvin Gaye

What's going on in our world of today

Stealing from each other, killing one another

Lying, cheating and still calling each other brother

Disillusioned by what our lives should really be

Misunderstanding that we're all born in sin, you and me

Forgetting each day to let live and let love

Forgetting to give all praises due to God up above

Everyone needs to take time out to pray

And ask God to forgive our sins each and everyday

To replace hate with peace and love wherever we can

Only then can we see what's going on all over the land

So for me this is what's really going on

We as a people must come together before all life is gone!!!

Yesterday

Yesterday is long gone and so very far behind

Yesterday is something only in our minds does it shine

Yesterday is when the elders had troubles far away

Yesterday I accept as the past so I live only for today

Someone said tomorrow is not promised and yesterday has past

Someone said right now is what's going on, so tell me how long can it last

I believe that a mixture of the past and the present in the world of today

Is all we need to endure, for the future belongs to only God I say

So why not live one day at a time and each moment experience the treasure

I believe our lives would be much easier, happier and full of God's love and pleasure!

You And I

You and I must make a pact

To be mindful of how we act

Toward each other no matter what

And not hold hatred down in our gut

We must understand that everyone is unique

And know that a change is what everyone seeks

With time and patience, with help from up above

We can conquer the hatred we feel and replace it with God's love

For only with God's guidance and his so many blessings

Will we understand living life together without ever guessing

We'll finally know what it is to live on this planet together

To love each other for who we are and not what we are for now and forever!!!

Santa Claus

Today while watching the news I heard that Santa Claus
arrived in a helicopter

They also talked about tax cuts and how the politicians were
eating out at Red Lobster

What happened to the days when the bells rang for Santa
Claus, his reindeer and sled

What happened to the belief in miracles and all the little
children went to bed

Waiting for that glorious morning to open all the presents
that Santa left under the tree

Asking questions about how he brought all the gifts down
the smoke filled chimney

Waiting day and night, trying to be good all for Christmas so
we'd be granted the ultimate blessing

Looking back and understanding that as a child I was
tricked, Santa in a helicopter that's a new lesson

Without the holidays Thanksgiving and Christmas Day
what else is there to really look forward to

Without giving thanks for so many blessings and being
thankful for Jesus' birth, just to name a few

So for me Christmas has somehow lost the true spirit and
has been misunderstood by all

We must always remember God's blessings, don't forget to give thanks and bring back Rudolph the Red Nose Reindeer driving Santa Claus!!!!

About the Poet:
Willa D. Jones

Fifty-four year old Willa Denise Jones sells *Street Vibes* newspapers today because the Vibe is what saved her life!

Being homeless and on the street all alone, reading the paper made her understand the she wasn't really alone. So she got involved and started writing poetry for the paper in order to be able to share her story with others. Writing about all the things she has been through and how God didn't give up on her.

Today by the support of different organizations such as: The Off The Street Program, Cincinnati Homeless Coalition, The Daily Bread, St. John Franciscan and St. Vincent DePaul, she was able to obtain housing for the first time in five years. The first being at the Anna Louise Inn on Lytle Place from one-room efficiency to the one bedroom apartment she now has.

Knowing how far she has come and how blessed she has been, she now takes pride in being a Contributing Writer for the Street Vibe Paper. When she is not writing she does 500 to 1000 piece jigsaw puzzles as a hobby which make declarations for her walls.

For now she will continue her mission of writing for the paper and continues to pray that God gives others the insight, the strength and understanding of living life one day at a time as he has so gracefully blessed her with.

Made in the
USA
Monee, IL